This Thing call LOVE

By: Areail Bowman

Sunflower Press Publishing Company

Acknowledgments :

Thank you for giving me a reason to get up every morning and continue to write .

-My son

You opened up my eyes and made me realize what love was and I appreciate that , so i'm dedicating this to you .
-Anonymous

In a world filled with flowers be a SUNFLOWER .

men stop letting this elementary school
heartbeat dictate your future relationship.

Can't be afraid to lose something that wasn't
yours in the first place.

i self-sabotage my current happiness because
of my past experiences. .

We don't talk no more and I think it's better that way

You showed me your true colors and I still
ignored that shit because I loved you.

you're biggest problem is
you can't be alone
you crave attention from others
crave companionship
crave the feeling of being needed by someone

AB. POETRY

Why did you tell me to wait for you , if you were
going to pick someone else ? Why have me wait
if I wasn't first on you're list ?

A B . P O E T R Y

i thought overthinking was killing me
whole time it was trying to save me from getting
hurt again.

I'm bout to start playing your game
and
let's see which one of us wins .

I'm just going to sit back and let karma handle
your ass.

when he lay his head on your inner thigh while
he tasting you're nectar.

انت حطمت قلبي

was just picking out our wedding colors
now i'm scrolling through my Photos deleting
any memory of you

AB. POETRY

I'm so tired of basic sex
can you tie me up and call me princess?

If you really love someone you're always make
time out your busy day for them.

when you are mentally , physically and
emotionally attractive to someone the sex is soo
much better .

i guess i'll see you in another lifetime
because in this one we ain't meant to be

A B . P O E T R Y

i'm just going to sit back and let karma handle
you

Continuing to love you is killing be slowly
but i still veer my heart away from all the
negative evocation moments we share.

AB. POETRY

I asked 2021 to be easy on me since the last 4
years has been cruel to me . 2021 has been
beating my ass these last 5 months.

AB. POETRY

" Please be kind to me" she screams to the
universe
"why ?"
"because your all i have left "

A B . P O E T R Y

kisses are slow and passionate
you're lips parts and say i love you
kissing my shoulders, my back bone and my
arms
telling me "you are on punishment"

you loved me more then i loved myself
and you cared about me when i didn't give a
damn about myself .

HIM

i met you when i was still trying to find who I was , lost
in a relationship with someone i thought i loved
we were just friends but we had so much in common
we talked every day
got to know each other
i told you things i didn't tell my boy friend
i was falling in love with you and i knew you felt the same
but i was in the relationship
you weren't in school , didnt have a job , you were in the streets
i was in school straight A's and had things you didn't have
but i made sure everytime i had something would you had it to
one day everything changed
i couldn't hold back the feelings i had
i told you
and you felt the same
actually you felt it stronger then me
i never had sex
yyou never had sex
 we had sex
together
the emotions was so heavy in that room
i felt the love
happy to be with you
we were together
but it was a problem
i still had a boyfriend
should i tell him ?
NO
he watched as i continue to be with my boyfi
not leave him like i promised
i didn't know that i was breaking him in the ʀ

my spirit wants to be healed
my mind wants peace
my body wants sex
my heart wants love

How do you want loyalty but YOU'RE
NOT FUCKING LOYAL?

. She's a angle during the day
But a devil in the bedroom

A B .   P O E T R Y

Playlist:

Jhene Aiko -Triggered
Tink -What is Real
Lyre Jennings- Must be nice
Sam Smith -Too good at Goodbyes
Inayah -What are we
Jhene Aiko- New Balance
Giveon- Like I want You
Deborah Cox-We can't be friends
Giveon - Heartbreak Anniversary
Whitney Houston - I have nothing
Joe-I'd rather have a love
Jhené Aiko -Never call me
Russ - Losin Control
Avant ft Keke Wyatt - You & I

Made in the USA
Columbia, SC
26 June 2024

37565543R00020